Twelve Owls

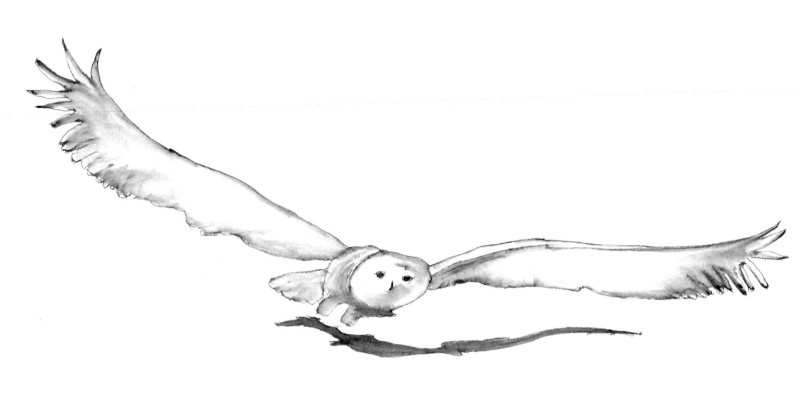

To Elesa:
Always embrace your
love of nature.
Owl the Best,
Laura Erickson

Twelve Owls

Laura Erickson

Illustrations by Betsy Bowen

UNIVERSITY OF MINNESOTA PRESS
MINNEAPOLIS • LONDON

The University of Minnesota Press gratefully acknowledges assistance provided for the publication of this book by the John K. and Elsie Lampert Fesler Fund.

Published by the University of Minnesota Press
111 Third Avenue South, Suite 290
Minneapolis, MN 55401-2520
http://www.upress.umn.edu

Library of Congress Cataloging-in-Publication Data
Erickson, Laura
Twelve owls / Laura Erickson ; illustrations by Betsy Bowen.
p.   cm.
ISBN 978-0-8166-7758-0 (hc : alk. paper)
1. Owls—Minnesota. 2. Owls in art. I. Bowen, Betsy. II. Title.
QL696.S8E75 2011
598.9'709776—dc23

2011023620

Printed in Canada on acid-free paper

Book design by Brian Donahue / bedesign, inc.

The University of Minnesota is an equal-opportunity educator and employer.

18 17 16 15 14 13 12 11   10 9 8 7 6 5 4 3 2 1

Thanks to my husband, Russell, who told his mom to get me binoculars and a field guide and was there when I saw my very first owls; to Gary Duke, who taught me to appreciate birds on the inside as well as the outside; and to the many birders and ornithologists who generously shared so much of their time and expertise. L.E.

Thanks to Ruth Harrison Lovejoy, my bird-loving grandmother. B.B.

Contents

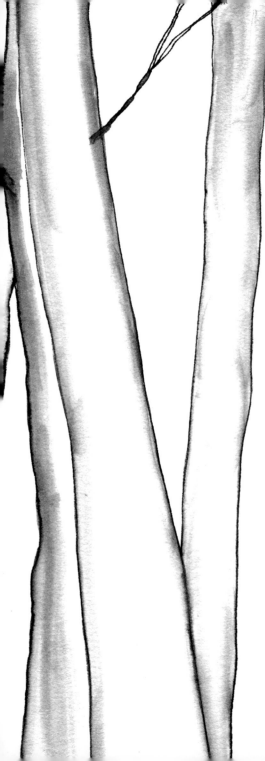

Artist's Note

Now, thanks to Laura Erickson, I know that owls are not only big but small. The color paintings in this book that open each essay are intended to show these owls at life-size. These paintings were made with acrylic paints on gessoed paper, and the drawings throughout the book were created with ink and a Rotring ArtPen and brushes with water on watercolor paper.

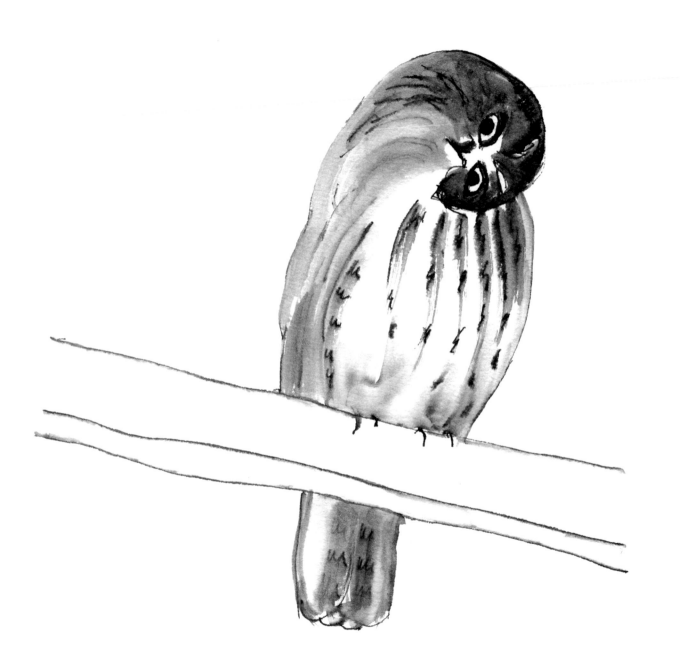

Introduction

If you are reading these words in the United States or Canada, there is an excellent chance that a wild owl is roosting or hunting or incubating eggs or brooding chicks less than ten miles from you at this very moment. If you are in Minnesota, chances are an owl is less than half that distance away from you. Of the twelve species of owls that can be found in the state, two are quite rare, four are primarily winter visitors, and another is declining, but the others are widespread year-round.

Owls are hardly abundant, but they are widely distributed, living in large forests, small woodlots, open prairie, agricultural areas, small towns, and major metropolitan areas. Despite their ubiquity, owls are exceptionally secretive. I lived the first twenty-four years of my life without seeing a single one. But once I became a birder and learned how to look for them, I saw my first three species within a month. A Snowy Owl flew right above my husband and me as we strolled along Lake Shore Drive in Chicago during our Christmas break in 1975. Right after we returned to Michigan State University in early January, I spied a Great Horned Owl roosting in

a popular campus woodlot. In the previous four years I had probably walked past this bird a dozen times without imagining such a magical creature could be right there. Two weeks later, some birders reported three Short-eared Owls on a farm field a couple of miles from the Michigan State campus. I stopped by several times over the next few days, and each time I easily found them roosting or hunting in the open.

Some common species eluded me, keeping me from growing complacent despite my beginner's luck. Several birders told me about an Eastern Screech-Owl that regularly roosted in a Wood Duck house, often poking its head out of the hole, along a particular trail in an arboretum. I checked dozens of times before I finally saw it. I expected to find screech owls at Picnic Point, a University of Wisconsin campus park that I visited almost daily before work when I lived in Madison. I consistently checked several nest boxes and a dozen woodpecker holes but never got a glimpse of one during five years of searching. Then, during the final week before we moved to Minnesota, a friend who had a tape player took me out one evening. We walked pretty much the same route I did every morning while he played screech-owl calls and found eighteen!

I didn't hear my first "Who cooks for you? Who cooks for you-all?" until I had been birding for four years, and never got a glimpse of a Barred Owl until a birding buddy brought me to a nesting pair. But with practice, I became good at imitating Barred Owls and now have good luck calling them in at least once every spring.

Many nights during the fall of 2010, a male Great Horned Owl hooted in my Duluth neighborhood, often perched atop my neighbor's large radio antenna. A female started responding to him in late November. I watched them calling many times, but when I walked through the neighborhood in daytime, scanning every conifer, I never spotted them without the help of squawking crows. Every speckle in an owl's plumage and every impulse in its brain help it to avoid detection.

Cryptic colors and the ability to sit still for hours allow owls to hide in plain sight. Prey species survive by listening and looking out for danger, and in response, owls are designed to elude detection by the keenest eyes and ears, even as they close in for the kill. Their soft, dense feathers muffle sounds, and their flight feathers bear a stiff comb at the leading edge, breaking even the softest whoosh into dozens of even softer whooshes.

Hidden behind their facial disks, owl ears are huge. Their hearing is about ten times more acute than a human's. They can pick up high-pitched rodent squeaks as well as their own deep hoots. We intuitively grasp that owls owe their success as predators to stealth. But that's just half the reason why an owl's flight is silent. Their ears are located on the sides of their head; during flight, the ears are right next to their flapping wings. Silent, relatively slow flight enables an owl to keep listening to even the tiniest rodent's sounds as it flies toward it. Many rodents spend winter hidden under snow; throughout the year, some live almost entirely within grassy tunnels. The first glimpse an owl gets of a vole is often after the little rodent is firmly grasped in its talons.

Because owls often strike without seeing their prey, their ears must continuously track the prey's distance as well as its direction. If an owl misjudges the distance by even an inch, it can come up with empty talons or crash into the ground. To gauge the distance as it flies toward prey, an owl's ears are crooked, one set lower and farther forward than the other. This asymmetry carries sound to one ear a split second before it reaches the other, and the owl's brain does the calculations even as it closes in.

Owl feet are also adapted for nocturnal hunting. Soft feathers cover the muscular toes down to the claws, contributing to silent flight as well as providing some insulation. Like many birds, owls have three front toes and one hind toe, but unlike most birds, one front toe is opposable. That and the owl's relatively long claws widen its grasp, giving it margin for error.

Owls seldom pursue running or quick-flying prey. They mostly hunt animals that are sitting or walking about. For example, Great Horned Owls often take roosting crows at night, when the crows are helpless. But the very adaptations that make owls such supreme nocturnal hunters put them at a disadvantage against crows in daytime. The features that make owls stealthy also make them slower and less maneuverable.

The sight of an owl alarms many birds as much as the sight of a snake does. Indeed, many people share that alarm—every human culture has folklore and mythology about owls, usually connecting them with death. When a squirrel or rabbit detects an owl, it often freezes in place or hides. When a songbird detects an owl in the daytime, it makes an alarm call and starts scolding it. Birds recognize alarm calls by their own and other species, and gang up to "mob" the owl together. Chickadees, robins, and vireos are exceptionally aggressive against small owls. Jays and crows tend to be most aggressive toward larger owls. I've seen a robin draw blood attacking an Eastern Screech-Owl, and watched both a crow and a Blue Jay peck the head of a roosting Great Horned Owl and come up with blood on the beak. If they drive the owl away before nightfall, the owl won't be able to observe where they go to roost. But unless mobbing birds get extremely aggressive, an owl is usually safer sitting tight and enduring the taunts. If it does take off, chances are one or two of the marauding birds will follow anyway.

The retinas of owl eyes are huge and packed with rods, essential for detecting movement and shapes in darkness. The retinas of many owls also have cone cells, allowing them to detect at least some colors. Indeed, some owl feathers reflect ultraviolet light, indicating that the birds can see a wider spectrum than we can. The largest owls, weighing less than five pounds, have eyes about the size of a full-grown human's. Being forward facing, close together, and sunk into facial disks, owl eyes don't perceive quite as wide a field of view as our eyes do. Those of us with two eyes have a field of view of about 180 degrees, with about 120 degrees of binocular vision; an owl's field of view is about 110 degrees, with about 70 degrees of binocular vision.

The pupils of an owl's eyes dilate much wider than ours do, gathering more light to give them far better nocturnal vision. The trade-off is that their pupils can't close as much as ours. To block out bright sunlight, they usually keep their large upper eyelids partly or mostly closed. Their facial disks also provide some shade from above. When we spot an owl in daytime, it may appear to be sleeping, but its eyes are actually open a slit, watching our every move.

Beneath thick feathers, an owl's neck is surprisingly

long. Its fourteen cervical vertebrae (twice as many as we have) allow it to hold its body perfectly still while smoothly and quickly swiveling its head in every direction. Any owl can easily turn its head backward (180 degrees), and many can turn their head 270 degrees. Some wildlife rehabilitators and zookeepers report seeing large owls turn their heads almost 360 degrees. I have lived with and closely observed a screech owl for ten years but have never seen him turn his head more than 180 degrees. If he is tracking my finger as I rotate it around his head, when the finger goes farther than that, he instantly swivels his head the other way. As an owl roosts, the neck beneath the feathers is shaped rather like a question mark, but when the owl spots a potential mammalian predator, it can straighten its neck into an exclamation point, lengthening and narrowing its body and holding as still as a branch. If the ruse doesn't work and the intruder walks directly toward it, the owl may crouch and open its wings to appear as large as possible, moving its head side to side, hissing, and snapping its bill menacingly. If these actions don't send the intruder on its way, the owl will finally take off to find a more secluded spot.

An owl's exceptional ability to focus directly forward while concentrating on prey comes at a cost. Owls often collide with cars as they fly across roads, apparently oblivious to sound and movements from the sides.

To minimize owl deaths at roadsides, never toss apple cores, orange peels, bread crusts, or other food waste into roadside ditches. These foods attract mice, which in turn attract owls, sometimes dooming them.

An owl's facial disks, so helpful in hunting, become more of an impediment as the owl eats. Those feathers near its beak can get goopy and sticky when an owl tears apart its prey. Many owls swallow small animals whole or in just one or two clean bites. Animals as large as rabbits may be too heavy for an owl to carry in flight back to its nest. Biting off and swallowing the head before taking off lightens the load and provides the owl the energy to keep hunting for its family. When the owl has no hungry mouths waiting for food, it often eats on the ground right where it made the kill.

An owl's digestive juices aren't as acidic as those of hawks, and so can't dissolve bones, fur, or feathers. As a mouse passes into the first chamber of an owl's stomach, called the proventriculus or glandular stomach, acids dissolve the softer parts of the animal into a kind of mouse soup, with the bones and fur floating about like noodles. Then the slurry passes into the second chamber of the stomach, the gizzard or muscular stomach, where powerful muscles squeeze the liquid through a narrow passage into the intestines. The fur and bones remain in the gizzard. After liquid has been squeezed out of the gizzard, a tightly packed pellet of felted fur and bones remains, which the owl regurgitates. The contents of owl pellets are an accurate representation of the owl's diet. Indeed, agricultural researchers and wildlife biologists use owl pellets to learn what rodents are in an area. A Barn Owl's pellet (the kind most often dissected in classrooms) usually contains two or three entire mouse skeletons. Sometimes there is an additional skull or two. These are usually from the mice the owl caught last, after it was no longer so hungry.

Most owls hunt alone and tend to lead rather solitary lives outside the breeding season. But many of them do mate for life and may keep track of their mate in a nearby or overlapping territory even outside the mating season. Unlike hawks, owls appear to be rather affectionate toward their mates while nesting, occasionally preening one another. In most species, the female's body is larger than the male's, though the male's skull and vocal apparatus are larger in species whose males have deeper voices than the females.

Most owls live very short lives, never reaching their first birthday. But if an owl survives its first treacherous year, its life expectancy jumps. Wild Great Horned Owls bearing U.S. Fish and Wildlife Service leg bands have lived for twenty-eight years, and even little species such as screech owls may have life spans comparable to a dog's or cat's.

Throughout human history, owls have figured prominently in art, folklore, and mythology. Owls are among the very few animals that have a humanlike posture and a face with forward-facing eyes like ours. Their beak is situated right where our nose would be. That humanlike aspect contributes to owls' reputation for wisdom, which is enhanced by their ability to see in the dark. Owls are also considered vigilant because they are so alert at night.

Despite their fascinating ways, many people find owls frightening. In 1894, W. J. Broderip wrote in *Zoological Recreations*: "There are few animals that have been more suspiciously regarded than Owls. Their retired habits, the desolate places that are their favorite haunts, their hollow hootings, fearful shriekings, serpent-like hissings, and coffin-maker snappings, have helped to give them a bad eminence, more than overbalancing all the glory that Minerva and her own Athens could shed around them."

Even those of us who consider ourselves beyond superstition can feel a thrilling sense of magic and mystery when our eyes connect with those of an owl. As in many encounters with the natural world, the more we learn about owls, the more fascinating and yet mysterious they become. They live among us and go about their daily lives in plain view yet usually outside our awareness. This book provides an introduction to Minnesota's twelve species of owls. We hope it inspires you to venture out and discover their magic in your own world. ◉◉

Northern Saw-whet Owl

The October night was cold and still. The birder walked in the beam of a flashlight along a path through the woods to a tiny plywood shack that serves as a bird banding field station. The shelves were strewn with data notebooks, a few reference books, necklace-like strings of aluminum bands of various sizes, calipers, rulers, special pliers, and coffee mugs. Here and there, looking completely out of place, were plush animals that looked like Beanie Baby owls. Suddenly one of them turned its head and looked the birder straight in the eye. With a start she realized that these weren't toys. They were Northern Saw-whet Owls.

Saw-whet owls can be found anywhere in Minnesota during winter and in all but the extreme southwestern corner of the state during the breeding season, so it seems surprising that so many of them migrate. But bird banders at Hawk Ridge in Duluth capture well over five hundred every autumn, catching several dozen on the best October nights. On the night of October 7–8, 1989, an astonishing 292 were caught and banded, and an additional one was caught that already wore a leg band.

The owls are trapped in mist nets, which look like badminton nets constructed of fine threads. While these nets are open, researchers examine them every few minutes to untangle and remove any owls. Time is of the essence when banding birds, which must be removed from the net, measured, recorded, banded, and released in short order to prevent their becoming too stressed. During heavy migration periods, sometimes more birds are caught than can be processed immediately. In these cases, hawks are restrained in tubes that immobilize them and keep them in the dark, which calms them and protects them from injury until the bander can attend to and release them. Not so with saw-whet owls. Banders often just place them on shelves in the banding field station to wait their turn. The tiny owls sit placidly, like fluffy Miss Marples quietly but sharply observing everything around them. After being banded and released back into the night, rarely one will fly back into the station, perhaps not yet satisfied that it had taken in every detail.

This tiniest owl in Minnesota measures barely eight

inches from the tip of its blunt tail to the top of its rounded head. Males weigh about three ounces, roughly the same as a robin. Females are a bit heavier. The soft plumage, round shape, and apparent tameness endear these owls to humans, who find even their fierce yellow eyes adorable, staring out of such tiny faces.

There is more to an owl than meets the eye—at least a human eye. Newly molted Northern Saw-whet Owl feathers that seem simple shades of brown and white appear bright pink under a black light; bird eyes are sensitive to ultraviolet (UV) wavelengths and see this as a color. As feathers fade with exposure to sunlight, the UV color degrades, making older feathers pale and dull compared to newly molted ones. Banders equipped with a black light have a simple way to compare relative ages of a saw-whet's flight feathers to determine the bird's age.

Scientists are still trying to tease out the evolutionary value of ultraviolet coloration in feathers. As birds grow older, their experience tends to make them better parents and thus more desirable mates, so saw-whets may use UV patterns the way banders do, to figure out how old prospective mates might be. Because feathers slowly degrade in sunlight, birds with the brightest UV levels in their oldest feathers may be better at finding good cavities to stay out of the sun—another thing to consider in a potential mate. And the intensity of the UV coloration in a new feather can be an indicator of health and diet quality during molt, so again this coloration, which we can't see without technology, may help saw-whets identify the best providers among potential mates.

Outside of a banding station, the simplest way to see a wild saw-whet owl is to listen for a flock of chickadees making agitated scolding calls. To them, the owl is a vicious serial killer who must be banished from the area. Usually the owl sits tight, and often the chickadees move on before a robin, jay, or crow notices. Unlike mobbing chickadees, larger, more aggressive songbirds often physically attack small owls. If the saw-whet keeps its eyes almost completely closed, the mobbing birds may lose interest and move on. Roosting owls may appear to be sleeping, but their eyes are invariably open a slit as they watch our every move.

Saw-whet owls spend most days safely hidden in tree cavities. If a saw-whet is discovered by a chickadee when the owl is peeking out of a cavity, the little predator simply backs down into the hole, disappearing from sight. When a saw-whet is in an unfamiliar area and hasn't yet found a cavity, or if its cavity has been lost to a competitor or the tree destroyed in a storm, the owl may be forced to roost in the open, and some saw-whets seem to prefer sleeping in the open at least part of the time. In winter they may use the same roost site for many days in a row, so another way to discover a saw-whet is to search the ground beneath conifers for pellets and the "whitewash" from their droppings, and then scan the branches above. With practice in the right habitat, some birders become quite adept at finding these elusive creatures.

While saw-whet owls are virtually immobile by day, they are surprisingly animated at night. While searching for prey, they move not just their heads but their whole bodies every which way. During spring when males make their steady "co-co-co-co-co" advertising call, they move forward with every *co* as if imitating a cuckoo clock. The monotonous, steady tone, which sounds surprisingly like the warning beep of a truck backing up, carries as far as a thousand feet in forests and more than twice that over water.

Call-count censuses and fall banding show cycles of abundance and scarcity in saw-whets, but pellet and roosting owl searches indicate that populations are fairly stable. The conflicting results may be partly because breeding saw-whets call much more often when prey is plentiful, making them seem more abundant or scarce than they really are. And even though many more migrate when food is scarce, individuals remaining behind may make populations appear more stable than they are.

Saw-whet owl pairs normally remain monogamous during the nest season, but when prey and nest sites are abundant, they are sometimes polygamous. Mated birds preen each other, but there is no evidence that the pair bond lasts more than one season, probably because so many of them wander about during winter and so aren't likely to be in the same area come spring. Females select the nest cavity and incubate the three to seven eggs, remaining on the nest constantly except for one or two

brief trips in early evening to defecate and spit out a pellet. Males provide all the food for the female and nestlings until the youngest owlet is about eighteen days old, when the female leaves the nest. At this point, some females start hunting for the young, and some move on. A few of those may even start a new nest with another male.

The only place darker than deep forest on a moonless night is inside a tree cavity in that same dark forest, but nestling saw-whet owls are surprisingly easy to feed in the dark. They make a chirrup call while begging that helps the mother locate them, and white facial feathers that reflect even the tiniest rays of starlight form a V pointing directly toward their hungry mouths.

During the time the female stays inside the nest with the young, she keeps the cavity clean, but her young do not learn basic sanitation skills from observation. After mom moves out, pellets, feces, and rotting excess prey build up in a thick layer before the owlets finally fledge.

Unlike most owls, saw-whets are fairly good fliers from the time they first leave the nest. The brood stays fairly close together, fed by their father and occasionally their mother for another month or so as they develop their own hunting skills. Then the family disperses, and each owl, full grown yet still tiny, is on its own in the great big world. ◎◎

Eastern Screech-Owl

Two Eastern Screech-Owls were sleeping side by side, wings touching, on a frozen Valentine's Day morning. Their feathers were fluffed against the cold, their eyes closed, and their heads tilted down a bit as if resting their chins on their chests. It was bright and sunny outside, but inside the roost box it was peaceful and dark.

They were a well-matched duo. Like most Eastern Screech-Owl pairs, they were the same age, both almost four years old. They were skilled hunters who had spent so much time together that they knew exactly what the other one was up to even when they were hunting in different parts of the woods. Now, comfortably roosting together, their shared body heat made their winter roost box warm and cozy.

Suddenly they woke with a start as a loud, rhythmic hammering erupted. A Downy Woodpecker in the neighborhood had decided that this particular Wood Duck box produced the loudest sound anywhere on his territory. Several times a day he would fly in and start pounding away. The female owl, the larger and more irritable of the two, climbed to the entrance hole and stuck her head out, startling the woodpecker in mid-drum. He flew off.

The sun was shining directly on the box now, warming the screech owl's head feathers, so she stayed put, dozing a bit. Gradually her stomach started churning, and up came a pellet, which she spit out on the ground below. Most of her pellets contained the indigestible remains of just one or two mice, but last night was an exceptional hunting night, and so this was a big pellet—the leftover fur, bones, and teeth of three mice. She needed the calories after two bad nights. A huge blizzard had kept her and her mate in the box three nights ago. The following night was clear, but the winds were fierce, and she wasn't hungry enough to face that. Her mate did go out for a little while and caught one plump mouse. He bit off the front third and swallowed it right where he killed it. Then, because the oncoming breeding season was affecting his hormone levels, he brought the rest to her. Had anyone examined the pellets they produced yesterday, they would have found half of a mouse's bones in each.

In winter, most of her pellets and those of her mate

fell into their roost cavity. The bottom of this Wood Duck box was thick with them, cushioning and insulating the floor. She was much more careful not to spit pellets into her nesting cavity than into her winter roost.

She wasn't entirely satisfied with this roost. It was a Wood Duck box, rather large for their nesting requirements. Woodpecker holes and other natural cavities stay more humid and keep a more constant temperature than artificial nest boxes. Her mate kept a sharp lookout for undefended cavities on their territory, and most winters they alternated among three or even four for roosting. This year starlings had taken over the best ones.

A couple weeks ago, her mate had dispatched a starling who had been roosting in a flicker hole. He had checked out the cavity and roosted in it twice since eating its former tenant. Several days ago he had even stored a couple of mice in it — a clear sign that he thought it might be a good choice for a nesting site this year. Her own rising hormone levels were making her restless. She would move into it in a few days, when they started courting in earnest. Hunkering down in a good nest cavity for a week or two seemed just the trigger she needed to start producing eggs.

She and her mate had settled in this city park when they first got together almost three years before. That first year they tried to nest in a different flicker hole, but she got skittish when starlings kept trying to take over, and she finally gave up. The second year her mate found a Pileated Woodpecker hole that turned out to be ideal. They successfully raised all four chicks that year, and last year they raised five more healthy owlets in it. But a storm last fall knocked the tree down. Fortunately, this happened after the young had all fledged, and none of them happened to be roosting in it at the time.

For all its flaws, this box was in the perfect location for a winter roost, close to the city zoo, where mice could always be found raiding the zoo animals' food troughs. The first year, her mate had bruised his wing colliding with a bar on the giraffe's cage and started avoiding the zoo, but after she figured out where to perch on the top of enclosures so she could drop down on mice safely, the zoo became her favorite hunting ground. In summer, the security lights drew in plenty of big moths too.

She was dozing again when her mate got restless and started jostling against her. She pulled in her head and retreated to the floor while he took a turn with his head sticking out. Any passing birders would not have realized this was a different individual. Eastern Screech-Owls come in two colors, gray and red, which differ genetically in much the way people with blond or brown hair differ, but like the vast majority of screech owls in Minnesota, these individuals were both gray. In screech owls, gray feathers tend to be thicker and more durable than red ones and probably provide better insulation; those with gray plumage have much higher survival rates during cold weather. One Baylor University researcher reports that red Eastern Screech-Owls in central Texas are increasing in number. Four decades ago they comprised about 7 percent of the population; in 2009 it was closer to 15 percent. He predicts that the red ones will become more numerous as climate-warming trends continue.

No passing birders noticed the owls, but suddenly a Blue Jay did and started squawking. The owl pulled back into the box, sat beside his mate again, and started preening the feathers on her face. She moved her head toward him and closed her eyes as he drew the feathers through his beak, and after a minute or two, she took a turn preening him. Preening one another's facial feathers helps cement the bond between owls. Young screech owls remain in the nest for a full month after hatching, and after they fledge, the family stays close together for at least two months longer. This mutual preening among family members strengthens their bonds, keeping the young with their parents and promoting their survival until they have all the skills necessary to survive independently.

When parents can't find enough food for their nestlings, the smallest may die. But in 75 percent of nests unmolested by predators, all the young survive to fledge. Nests in urban areas are far less likely to suffer predation than those in wilder areas.

Small cavity-nesting owls in Texas and Mexico occasionally carry live blind snakes to their nest, which seems to improve breeding success. The snakes, which are too small to eat screech owl eggs or chicks, do eat ant and fly larvae and pupae, reducing insect competition for stored food. Blind snakes aren't found in Minnesota, but screech owls in the north don't have to deal with as many insect pests as those in Texas do.

In late afternoon, the female climbed up to the entrance hole again and looked out for twenty minutes or so before her mate got restless. She stepped back, letting him take over the entrance. He studied everything going on around him as the sun slowly sunk. Crows were flying overhead, all headed southeast toward their roost. One by one, chickadees were disappearing into their cavities, and squirrels into their leafy shelters. One squirrel kicked off a twig as he jumped from branch to branch in a maple tree. The twig dropped into a little puddle of snowmelt with a welcome plop. The temperature was falling, but winter really was losing its sting.

Fifteen minutes after sunset, the male pulled out of the cavity to start his busy night. His mate soon followed. Wild Eastern Screech-Owls have survived fourteen years or more. Chances were excellent that this pair would be found together in these lovely woods for years to come. ◎◎

Burrowing Owl

The photographer was visiting an active prairie dog town in the Black Hills of South Dakota, snapping photo after photo of prairie dog antics. The little rodents were endlessly entertaining, but she seemed vaguely dissatisfied, often looking beyond the prairie dogs in search of something else. Finally, she spotted what she was looking for: a five-ounce owl sitting at the edge of a prairie dog burrow, its legs improbably long, its brilliant yellow eyes glittering in the sun.

Suddenly the bird looked sharply down and pounced on a big, fat dung beetle, popping it into its mouth. The photographer took dozens of shots before a harrier suddenly came up from nowhere and swooped directly toward the owl, sending it scurrying back into its burrow.

A very young prairie dog barely reached its burrow in time. The photographer wondered if its narrow escape from the harrier's talons only delayed the inevitable—if one day soon it would be taken by the Burrowing Owl. She needn't have worried. Burrowing Owls seldom, if ever, feed on the burrowing mammals they live with.

They prey on small rodents, lizards, and birds hunted at some distance from their subterranean homes. They do lure dung beetles closer to home by collecting mammal scat and depositing it all around the entrance to their burrow.

The Zuni name for the Burrowing Owl means "priest of the prairie dogs," because they so frequently nest and roost in empty prairie dog burrows. Early European settlers were convinced that Burrowing Owls nested with rattlesnakes, and a few books report this as fact. When alarmed inside their burrow, young Burrowing Owls make a sound very much like a rattlesnake, which naturally scares off a lot of potential predators and people before they investigate further. But rattlesnakes are every bit as much a predator on these little owls as they are on other small warm-blooded animals.

The Greek goddess Athena is often depicted holding in her hand or on her arm a close relative of the Burrowing Owl, the Little Owl, which was given the scientific name *Athene noctua* in 1769 by Italian naturalist Giovanni Antonio Scopoli to honor the relationship between

Athena and her owl. The Burrowing Owl's biggest claim to fame in American culture is being the subject of the Carl Hiaasen novel and movie *Hoot*.

Burrowing Owls live in a variety of dry, open, short-grass, treeless plains. The species is one of the few in America with two widely separated ranges. One population lives in Florida. The rest live in plains and deserts from California to the Dakotas, where they usually associate with burrowing mammals such as prairie dogs, ground squirrels, and badgers, taking over abandoned burrows. These western birds occasionally nest as far east as extreme western Iowa and Minnesota. Burrowing Owls were probably never common in Minnesota. Reports of them in recent decades have been very rare and scattered, centered mostly in and near the Glacial Ridge National Wildlife Refuge. The Burrowing Owl is the only owl listed as endangered in Minnesota by the Department of Natural Resources, its scarcity due to dwindling grassland habitat in the state.

Those in Florida, where burrowing animals are less abundant, tend to excavate their own burrows. Florida's Burrowing Owls occasionally roost in trees, perhaps because acceptable burrows are at a premium, but they always nest in some kind of burrow. Within both ranges, Burrowing Owls also live in developed areas such as golf courses, airports, vacant lots in residential areas, and fairgrounds. Some birding guidebooks direct birdwatchers to old cemeteries in the Southwest, where ground squirrels and Burrowing Owls scurry in and out of tunnels crisscrossing the graveyard. A fanciful birder seeing a Burrowing Owl perched atop a headstone or cross may wonder if the owl is thinking, "Alas, poor Yorick. He was my living room."

Most of the year, Burrowing Owls are nocturnal or crepuscular, but during nesting season when they have young to feed, they spend daylight hours catching insects and lizards, and nighttime hours catching rodents.

Unlike most owls, in this species the male and female are about the same size. Each male selects or excavates a burrow and then begins defending his territory and trying to attract a mate. Pairs in Florida and the Southwest remain together year-round, but those that migrate from farther north don't appear to maintain their pair bond beyond the nesting season. The female lays two to twelve eggs. Males in Florida often drop belly feathers to form what mimics a brood patch, but the underlying skin lacks the rich supply of blood that makes a true brood patch effective at incubating eggs. Throughout their range, only female Burrowing Owls incubate eggs or brood chicks. Males provide virtually all the food for their young, delivering it to the female to feed the chicks. In Florida, researchers have observed that when females die, their nestlings all starve despite the abundance of food their father brings, because he lacks the instinct to feed them.

Burrowing Owls have habits and physical adaptations that make them successful at living on and below ground. Lining the entrance to their burrow with mammal scat attracts dung beetles for them to eat and also masks the owls' odor, which may keep badgers, foxes, and other digging predators from discovering them. Adding manure also builds up a patch of higher ground, affording the owls a better view in their short-vegetation habitat. Their legs are unusually long for owls, giving them an even wider field of view. Burrowing Owls tolerate much higher levels of carbon dioxide than other owls, including cavity nesters, presumably because air exchange inside their long and winding burrows can be poor at best.

The few Burrowing Owls that appear in Minnesota are highly migratory. Every now and then, one appears far out of its range. One turned up in Duluth on May 31, 1997, which happened to be the St. Louis County Big Day, when birders throughout the state were combing the county for birds. Although this was before iPhones and electronic hotlines, and before most birders carried cell phones, the birding network managed to get the word out to a great many of the Big Day participants. Although the owl disappeared that afternoon and was never relocated, it was seen by a surprising number of birders who had never seen a Burrowing Owl in the state before and probably haven't since.

Although Burrowing Owls take advantage of burrows provided by humans in many areas, on balance people have been more of a hindrance than a help to the species. A study of one Florida population found that domestic cats accounted for 30 percent of the birds' deaths. As with several other owl species, collisions with automobiles are a major cause of mortality. Farming takes a toll on the bird and its habitat, especially when farmers evict prairie dogs and destroy their burrows. Pesticides can poison the birds directly and also reduce grasshoppers and other important food resources for them. Development in prairie areas has led to fire suppression and more shade trees, leading to an increase in Great Horned Owls, major predators of Burrowing Owls.

The Minnesota population is on the verge of disappearing. In 2007, only a single pair was discovered nesting anywhere in the state. They raised two owlets in a restored prairie at the Glacial Ridge National Wildlife Refuge. The Minnesota Department of Natural Resources, the Nature Conservancy, and the U.S. Fish and Wildlife Service are working together to restore prairie habitat to help this critically endangered species. ◎◎

Boreal Owl

The January predawn twilight was quiet and still except for the occasional creaking of a birch straining against the bitter cold. A tiny owl sat on a branch, quiet but not still, her head turning every which way, her eyes and ears straining to detect the slightest movement or sound. She hadn't eaten in almost two days, and hunger made her desperate. A sudden squeak caught her attention. She dropped her gaze just in time to see a deer mouse dart across the shallow depression in the snow at the base of the tree. She plunged at top speed, grabbed the mouse, bit it sharply at the base of its skull, and swallowed it with practiced efficiency. The mouse's warm body filled her stomach within three seconds of catching it. Two inches of tail drooped from her mouth for several minutes more before slipping out of sight. By the time the sun rose, she was roosting in an old Pileated Woodpecker cavity, safe for the day. She would emerge after sunset in search of enough calories to carry her through another day.

Other Boreal Owls were also desperately searching for food. One male cornered a flying squirrel on a back-yard feeder, but a split second before the owl could sink his talons into it, the little rodent squeezed through a narrow opening below the feeder's roof and found itself inside the feeder's storage hopper. The soft tail slipped out of the owl's grasp just as he wheeled and turned in mid-wing stroke, barely avoiding a crash. He flew to a nearby spruce to consider. The squirrel was frustratingly visible behind the hopper's glass side panel. It even sat up and ate a few seeds, as if taunting the hungry bird. The owl was torn between flying off in search of something easier and waiting it out.

Flying squirrels weigh 3 or 4 ounces, a little less than the average male Boreal Owl's 4.1 ounces, and they cling to life tenaciously. They are tricky even for healthy female Boreal Owls, averaging 5.9 ounces, to subdue. Battling one is difficult enough when the owl is in top condition. By January in a winter when mouse populations are low, many Boreal Owls are emaciated, their breast muscles atrophying and their strength ebbing. The odds for this owl were low, but the reward if he succeeded was a full stomach with enough meat left over, cached in his roost-

moisture from its breath condensing and freezing on the glass panel. Suddenly it squeezed out of the feeder and made a flying leap toward the trees opposite the owl as the owl took off after it. Just as they reached the spruce tree, the owl sunk his talons into the flying squirrel's lower back. The rodent twisted around and bit sharply into the owl, but its teeth caught nothing but feathers as the two fell to the ground and wrestled, the owl trying desperately to get in a lethal bite at the base of the skull even as the squirrel struggled equally desperately to keep that vulnerable area out of reach and look for any opportunity to escape. The owl's talons had caught the squirrel too low in the back for him to keep it under control, and the two of them grappled in the snow for a full ten minutes before the squirrel made a wrong move. The owl bit hard, and the battle was over.

He tried to take off with the squirrel but could barely lift its body an inch off the ground, so he simply dragged it behind the trunk. He would have started feasting right then, but birders were not the only witnesses to the battle. Two crows had silently flown in to observe the whole thing. Now they dropped to the ground and walked purposefully toward the owl, one heading toward him from the right side of the trunk, the other from the left. The little owl puffed up his feathers, clacked his beak, and hissed, but the crows didn't hesitate. They pulled the rodent from the owl's grasp and

ing cavity, to carry him through another night or two. So he waited it out.

When the sun rose, the owl was still perched in the little spruce, staring at the feeder. Suddenly a caravan of cars pulled into the driveway, and a group of birders piled out. They focused their binoculars and cameras on the owl but kept their distance. The flying squirrel had hunkered down in the feeder, its large nocturnal eyes growing more uncomfortable as the morning grew brighter, warm

dragged it a few inches away. He gave up and took off, exhausted and hungrier than ever. He landed in a thick spruce and closed his eyes. A chickadee spotted him and started scolding. It was going to be a long day.

Boreal Owls are safest when they spend daytime in a cavity, usually an abandoned Pileated Woodpecker hole. In response to low food availability in winter, the owls wander, often ending up in unfamiliar areas where they haven't yet discovered an undefended cavity. In these cases they roost in a tree, vulnerable to predators and the prying eyes of mobbing birds. Chickadees are little more than nuisances for a Boreal Owl, but their scolding alerts more dangerous species to the scene. Scolding chickadees also often signal birders that a small owl is nearby.

The birding community is ever on the alert for Boreal Owls. Because at least one or two of them appear most years in Duluth or Two Harbors, birders from throughout the United States gravitate to northern Minnesota in hopes of seeing one. The other three northern owls—the Snowy, Great Gray, and Northern Hawk Owls—are generally more predictable and easier to find, except during Boreal Owl "invasion years" when mouse populations crash farther north. But thanks to text messaging and various cell phone apps, a birder who chances upon a Boreal Owl can now get the GPS coordinates of the precise location out to hundreds of other birders within seconds.

Boreal Owls breed in boreal and sub-alpine forests throughout the Northern Hemisphere. They are the most abundant forest owls in Scandinavia, where they have been studied intensively. In North America, their breeding range is restricted mostly to Canada and Alaska, dipping into the Rocky Mountains and Cascades and barely into northern Minnesota. People didn't realize Boreal Owls nested in the state, or indeed anywhere in the Lower 48, until the spring of 1978, following a large winter "invasion," when Kim Eckert and Terry Savaloja heard fifteen different males calling along the Gunflint Trail. They discovered one male calling near what appeared to be a suitable cavity in a black spruce stump; in later searches, a female was discovered in the cavity, and then eggs. The pair raised five chicks.

After that exciting discovery, systematic Boreal Owl censuses verified more nesting in Cook, Lake, and extreme northeastern St. Louis Counties. Nests are still quite rare and often inaccessible, so most birders see Boreal Owls only during winter. The best years for birders tend to be the worst for the owls; during invasion years, a great many are found dead or dying. Unlike most birds, Boreal Owls have a tendency to draw close to human habitation when close to death. This behavior is not understood, but the phenomenon is not limited to Minnesota. Reports from the early 1900s include several of Boreal Owls spending daytime in igloos along the Agapuk River in Alaska and in barns in New Hampshire and Maine near Lake Umbagog. Desperate ones may mistake our windows as entries to shelter.

In April, when winter is drawing to a close, male Boreal Owls begin calling. Each male's ringing, staccato "hoo-hoo-hoo-hoo-hoo-hoo-hoo-HOO," which from a distance can be confused with a winnowing snipe, is produced to attract a mate after he has found a suitable nest site, most often an abandoned Pileated Woodpecker cavity. This call carries at least a mile. Males don't respond to recordings of this call, which apparently functions strictly to attract a mate and not to defend a territory. After a female accepts a cavity, the male switches to a softer, longer call through courtship until the female begins incubating.

Female Boreal Owls are much bigger than males, showing the most extreme relative weight difference of any North American owl. Pairs are monogamous during the breeding season. The male hunts while the female spends most of her time in the cavity until the young can be left alone. Pairs normally remain together for a single breeding season, but in years when winter hunting is good, both may remain in the same vicinity and end up pairing again the following year.

Boreal Owls have survived in captivity for fifteen years. Despite how difficult their lives are and how high winter mortality can be, one Boreal Owl banded in Idaho in 1990 as a nestling was recaptured and released eight years later, and it is quite likely that others have survived in the wild even longer. They may appear tiny and adorable to our eyes, but their fierce, tenacious hold on life is clearly a force to be reckoned with. ◎◎

Barn Owl

In August 1995, a small band of Minnesota birders were riding in two vans along an Arizona country road lined with soybean fields, en route between Green Valley and Madera Canyon. The sun had just risen, and the soft morning light filled them with hope. They would see at least a few good birds before breakfast back in Green Valley.

One of them spied what looked like a dead raptor dangling from a fence and called out. The golden back spangled with silvery flecks instantly identified it as a Barn Owl. Most of the birders had never seen a living Barn Owl, and even those that had wanted a closer look at the exquisite plumage, so they pulled to the side of the road and walked toward the fence. As they approached, the owl suddenly came to life, flailing its wings but hopelessly snagged on a barb. Two birders working together managed to disentangle it. One of the owl's pupils was fixed and dilated, and the bird was very weak. A birder with wildlife rehabilitation experience administered a few drops of Gatorade while another emptied a Styrofoam cooler and punched large holes in the cover.

It was just a little after six o'clock, so there was little they could do except bring the owl along to Madera Canyon with them. They found a pay phone and left a message on the answering machine of a vet clinic in Green Valley that they would bring the owl in at eight o'clock.

The headless pack rat on the ground beneath the fence provided evidence about what had happened. Apparently at some time during the night, this male owl had caught the rodent. He presumably ate the head and was carrying the rest back to his family when the barbed wire stopped him. Barn Owls tend to fly fairly low to the ground in the open, treeless country where they make their homes, and are often killed in collisions with fences, wires, and automobiles. Their legs are long, dangling at about fence height when carrying prey. In this case, the legs hit the top of the fence. The owl probably dropped the rat at the moment of collision and would have gotten away with nothing more than bruises and empty talons except that one barb snagged its leg. Against the owl's momentum, the barb sliced a two-inch tear in the skin and held the owl fast. In struggling and scraping against

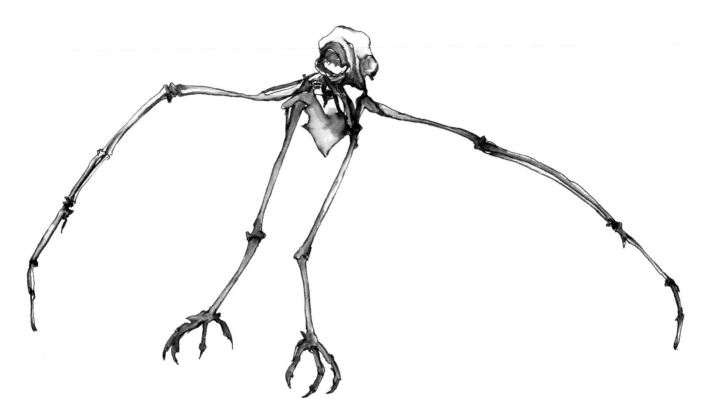

the fence during the night, the bird had lost a few body feathers, and now both legs were covered with cuts and abrasions.

Before the accident, the bird had apparently been in good health; it responded quickly to the electrolytes in the Gatorade. On hearing the phone message, the vet clinic receptionist immediately called in a wildlife rehabilitator, and at eight o'clock when the birders returned to Green Valley, the clinic was ready to receive them. The owl required fluids, antibiotics, steroids, and dissolv-

ing sutures but recovered quickly. Just four days later, he was released in the exact area where he had been injured. If the chicks weren't so young that the female was reluctant to leave them, and if hunting was reasonably good, it is possible that the pair raised most of them successfully despite the father's untimely accident. But had the birders not stopped to look at what appeared to be a dead bird, the owl would have died that day. By midmorning the temperature had climbed above 110 degrees.

Barn Owls are one of the "most-wanted" species

on Minnesota Ornithologists' Union trips to Texas and Arizona. Although the species is listed as nesting in Minnesota, only a handful of Minnesota birders have been lucky enough to see one in the state. Barely a dozen nests have been found in the state in the past half century, and because Barn Owls normally nest in barns on private property, concerns for both the landowner and the vulnerable nesting birds keep even these nest reports off birding hotlines.

Despite the Barn Owl's scarcity in the state, this rarest of all Minnesota owls is justifiably not listed on the state's endangered species list. Why? Barn Owls are not considered part of Minnesota's regularly occurring avifauna. There is no evidence that they were ever common in the state, which barely borders the species' distribution range.

Barn Owls are hard to find just about anywhere in the eastern half of America. Many ornithologists believe that they seldom lived in or even visited the upper Midwest before European settlers cleared the forests. In Great Lakes states, Barn Owl populations apparently reached their peak in the 1920s. They have been declining since the 1930s, and underwent large-scale declines between 1970 and 2000. During the same period, their numbers dramatically increased in the northwestern United States, where logging opened up habitat and irrigated agriculture led to an increase in the rodents Barn Owls feed on. These more abundant birds in Washington and Oregon provide most of the owl pellets purchased from biological supply houses for students to dissect.

Many people in states along the Atlantic and Pacific and in the South now set out nest boxes designed for Barn Owls, and more and more Barn Owls are taking advantage.

Ornithologists studying individual Barn Owls have seen little evidence that breeding adults migrate. Banded nesting birds tend to remain in the same general area year-round. But at migration hot spots such as Cape May, New Jersey, and along Lake Erie in Ohio, Barn Owl observations are significantly higher during spring and fall than in winter or summer. Barn Owl young can wander more than a thousand miles from where they were hatched, and unpaired adults and those whose nesting area has been altered may also wander widely. Whether these dispersal movements are a form of migration is a matter of semantics.

Barn Owls nest in cavities in a wide variety of trees, and also on cliffs and rock outcrops, in caves, and on river and arroyo banks. They also use a great many human structures. In addition to nest boxes, they can be found in or on church steeples, barn lofts, crevices in houses and other buildings, drive-in movie screens, and haystacks. One New Jersey study found that 50 percent of the population nested in tree cavities and 31 percent in nest boxes. In some areas, nearly 100 percent of resident Barn Owls now nest in nest boxes.

Although Barn Owls are extremely rare in Minnesota, birders can, in the comfort of their own homes, get close-up looks at nesting pairs and their growing young via the Internet, because the owls nest so readily in places where nest cams can be set up to provide live streaming video of their activities. Adults and children alike thrill at watching their activities as a pair raises five to seven young.

Barn Owls breed fairly readily in captivity and so have been subjects of a great deal of research. Through laboratory studies we know that they can successfully capture a mouse in absolute darkness. Unlike most species, female Barn Owls are more colorful than males, their golden brownish chest spotted with black. In laboratory tests, when a female's spots were experimentally removed, her mate fed their nestlings at a lower rate than if her spots were left alone. Heavily spotted females get fewer parasitic flies and may be more resistant to parasites and diseases. Researchers speculate that males can gauge a female's fitness by looking at these spots.

Over their entire range, on every continent except Antarctica, Barn Owls can be found on or in man-made structures, so people of many cultures are familiar with them. Their eerie sounds, a variety of screeches and hisses, and their ghostlike flight probably contributed greatly to folklore about owls as harbingers of death. When people and an owl collide, a death often does follow, but the death is virtually always the owl's. ◎◎

Short-eared Owl

The Short-eared Owl sat on her nest on a warm morning in late May, incubating two eggs and brooding two chicks. She had a pleasantly full belly—last night her mate had delivered an amazing seven voles. All but one were quite small, but even a tiny vole can provide three or four mouthfuls for newly hatched owlets, and the two chicks that had hatched so far were just four and two days old. After they had eaten their fill, there were plenty of leftovers for her.

It was a clear day, but she was shaded from the morning sun and protected from view in all directions by tall, fresh green grasses. Her nest was tucked within a shallow depression. Her mate occasionally flew directly over as if checking on his family, but right then he was sitting on a fence post a distance away.

Her older chick's eyes were already open. Just slits so far, but everything was right on schedule. One egg beneath her had been vibrating for hours as the chick within scraped its egg tooth against the shell—that chick could pop out any moment. And the chick inside the other egg was making high-pitched cheeps, so that egg was definitely fertile. Everything was going beautifully despite her late start. If the food supply held steady, in about a month, four young Short-eared Owls would be starting to fly. She and her mate would teach them to hunt on their own over this beautiful marsh, and by late summer they would scatter into the wider world.

This female was four years old. She had raised her first two broods in a marshy field a hundred miles from here, but when she returned to the area in March, it was changed beyond recognition. The soft marsh grasses that had provided tunnel systems for meadow voles seemed to have vanished. The field had actually been plowed under, and the thawing mud didn't seem to hold much food. She darted at both a Killdeer and a robin as she surveyed her old territory; she missed both. The pond that usually sang with frogs had been drained. The cattail stand that often provided young, tasty muskrats or a slow-witted rail was gone too. A huge, noisy tractor plowed through, and she flew off without looking back. She never learned if her mate had survived the winter.

She wandered miles and miles, scrutinizing the landscape and occasionally seizing a meal as she searched for a satisfactory but unguarded territory. She reached this field at dusk, right as a handsome male swooped through the air performing his splendid sky dance. He made a long series of soft tooting calls as he flew a hundred feet up while rapidly beating his elegant wings, showing off the conspicuous dark "comma" at the wing bend. Then he dropped at high speed, clapping his wings ten times or so. She called back to him, and that was that. He was getting a late start this breeding season, too, and they needed to start nesting as soon as possible.

She sat tight, feeling the chicks moving beneath her. The older one was an active little thing. Suddenly she felt the vibrating egg crack open. She lifted herself up and peeked down to see a wet little chick. She tossed the small end of the shell out of the nest. The larger end of the shell was still mostly sticking to the chick, but after the little guy rested a bit, he would wriggle out, and she would toss that away too.

She was starting to hear an odd, distant roar. A big green machine was moving along at the far end of the field. It was a safe distance away, but it made her nervous. It moved in a straight line along the far end of the field. When it got to where the road cut through, it didn't keep going—it turned around and moved along another line, this one a bit closer. It seemed to scare up her mate, who took flight and landed a little nearer to her.

The newly hatched chick suddenly moved again and managed to separate himself from the eggshell, which broke into a few pieces. She tossed the shell fragments out of the nest. The mower kept roaring along, turning and going the opposite direction whenever it reached an end of the field, coming ever closer, but she held firm. The roaring was scaring a lot of animals on that side of the field. Her mate grabbed a small rodent that had scurried away from the mower right toward him. He carried it straight to her and flew off again, this time in the opposite direction of the mower. She gave fairly big chunks to the oldest chick, smaller pieces to the second, and one tiny morsel to the newly hatched chick. Some of his down feathers were still wet, stuck against his skin, but his back and the top of his head were starting to look properly fluffy, and he seemed strong and healthy. When the owlets had filled their stomachs, all three went to sleep.

The mower kept going back and forth, back and forth. Gulls and crows were landing on the field where it had passed, picking up mangled chicks and eggs from other ground nests. The mower passed her at close range, and she could see how its huge blades chopped and crushed the soft meadow grasses and flowers. Bobolinks, sparrows, and meadowlarks flew up from their nests in a panic. Now the mower passed by much too close for comfort, its roar deafening, but she held tight even as it passed within five feet of her. At the end of the row, it turned around, this time headed straight for her. She didn't move as the roaring grew ever louder. She finally took off when the blades were less than a wing stroke away. A crow flying behind the mower dropped down to where her nest had been.

The Short-eared Owl has been listed as a species of special concern by the Minnesota Department of Natural Resources since 1984. Once widespread throughout the state except in the extreme northeast and southeast corners, it is now uncommon to rare, with most summer records limited to the northwestern corner of the state. It breeds in expansive native grasslands, marshes, and open peatlands, all declining habitats that continue to dwindle due to development, cultivation, and drainage. It also occasionally nests in grain fields and pastures, but because nests are built on the ground and the nest cycle lasts two full months, eggs and chicks are exceptionally vulnerable to disturbance by plowing, mowing, and agricultural pesticides.

Short-ears wander widely in search of food and habitat and are perhaps the most nomadic owl species in the world. They are found on every continent except Australia and Antarctica, and also on a great many oceanic islands, such as the Galápagos and Hawaiian Islands. These island systems didn't break away from continents, drifting away with plants and animals already present. They are volcanic, so all wildlife on them was carried there by wind or waves, swam or flew there on their own power, or were introduced by humans. Hawaii is more than eighteen hundred miles from the nearest continent. The only land mammal to colonize it on its own is the Hawaiian Hoary Bat. A few birds found their way and colonized the islands too. And when the Polynesians first arrived, there was already a population of Short-eared Owls.

The probability of at least two individual owls belonging to the same species but opposite sexes wandering to the exact same island in the middle of the vast ocean during the same brief lifetime (the oldest wild Short-eared Owl on record, from Europe, lived twelve years nine months) seems staggering. For them to not just survive the flight but to also be healthy enough to reproduce after such a long journey, with no resting places or opportunities to feed over the ocean, seems astonishing. That they not only did survive but established a viable population is downright miraculous. People have since introduced rats, providing more prey, but those same rats are scourges for ground-nesting birds, including Short-eared Owls. Introduced Barn Owls compete for food, and introduced mosquitoes carry diseases. No matter how far Short-eared Owls wander, people have made life harder for them, but so far they are holding their own. As long as they can find replacement habitat when they are evicted from nesting areas, and as long as enough of them can raise their young to independence, these splendid little owls will continue to share the planet with us. ◎◎

Long-eared Owl

During the last week of October 1991, a storm system so huge that it was nicknamed "the Perfect Storm" raged over the Atlantic Ocean. The magnitude of the system blocked the normal west-to-east storm patterns over the eastern half of the United States, forcing a huge low-pressure system from the Gulf of Mexico to rush north instead of east. Between October 31 and November 3, the resulting storm dumped 28.4 inches of snow on the Twin Cities and 36.9 inches of snow on Duluth in what Minnesotans will long call "the Halloween Storm."

So many meteorological records were set and so many dramatic stories emerged about the difficulties people faced after the unprecedented storm that little notice at all was taken about avian fatalities, but several Duluthians digging out after the storm were disconcerted to find frozen raptors, mostly Long-eared Owls, buried in the snow. The storm occurred at the peak of their migration. Right when these ten-ounce owls were most weary of traveling, they reached an area where the snow was too deep to plunge through to get mice, and many died of starvation. Fortunately, the Halloween Storm of 1991 is unlikely to be repeated. Usually Long-eared Owl migration occurs at the ideal time for them to find plenty of food along the way.

Of Minnesota's common and widespread owl species, long-ears may be the least often seen by birders. Many books and articles say they live in forests, and sure enough, the vast majority of sightings of them are in thick stands of trees, where they roost and nest. But year-round, Long-eared Owls hunt over grasslands, shrublands, and wide forest openings, much as Short-eared Owls do. It is possible that some Long-eared Owls hunting in twilight are even mistaken for Short-eared Owls, which are paler and less streaked below but share a dark, comma-like wrist mark. Birders spotting an owl with a wrist mark hunting above a field in low light may jump to the conclusion that it is a short-ear simply because so many field guides imply that the only alternative in this habitat is the Northern Harrier.

Long-eared Owls normally hunt on the wing, coursing back and forth across an open area, often less than six feet above the vegetation. They sometimes hover, and during windy conditions may hunt from perches. Like Barn Owls, they have exceptionally acute hearing; in captivity they can capture prey in complete darkness. Their vision in low light is also as good as that of other North American owls. Even in daylight many rodents in open areas stay completely hidden in tunnels or below vegetation, so hunting by ear makes it much easier to catch the deer mice and meadow voles that constitute most of their diet.

Long-eared Owls spend daytime roosting in trees. When one notices a person or other disturbance, it erects its feather tufts, closes its eyes all but a slit, stretches to make itself surprisingly tall, and holds utterly still. With luck, the intruder won't notice it blending in with the branches and will eventually move away. But if the intruder starts to approach, the owl will suddenly crouch with its head lowered, wings drooped, and feathers ruffled. Then it will open its eyes wide and move its head back and forth in a menacing way as it hisses, snaps its bill, and makes a variety of alarm calls. This usually scares off most people and potential predators, but if the intruder draws any closer, the owl will finally take off and move to another roost site.

Like Short-eared Owls, Long-eared Owls are sociable with their own kind. Several individuals may be found hunting on a field at the same time, and nests may be spaced closer than fifty feet apart. Long-ears often form communal roosts in winter, a dozen or more birds roosting near one another in a single stand of trees, two or more sometimes perched on the same branch. These communal roosts simplify the process for males and females to find one another and pair up during the winter, but some males move to suitable nesting areas more than a week before attracting mates.

In March and April, males produce their advertising call, a series of from ten to more than two hundred evenly spaced hoots, which can be heard more than half a mile away. Both sexes make a variety of other vocalizations, including sharp calls that from a distance sound like barking dogs.

Early in the nesting season, males perform their courtship flight, alternating deep wing beats with gliding as each one zigzags around and through a grove of trees that seems suitable for nesting. During this flight, they make occasional loud sounds called wing clapping, which can be heard a hundred yards away. Long-eared Owls make these single whiplike sounds at irregular intervals, unlike Short-eared Owls, which wing-clap in a rapid series.

When a male attracts a female to his grove, she searches for a suitable stick nest, usually built a year or two before by a crow or hawk. The female may sit in two or more nests on her mate's territory before making a final choice. There is little evidence that she modifies the nest or brings any material to it, though some belly feathers dropping from her brood patch may remain in the nest. She begins incubating as soon as she lays the first egg; clutches average four or five eggs, laid at two-day intervals. As in other owl species, the female Long-eared Owl has all the incubation responsibilities; her mate's job is to provide food for her and, after they hatch, the chicks. When hunting is good, the pair stockpiles food at the nest. The extra stores help when the young get bigger and require more calories.

Females sit tight all day, virtually never leaving the white, glossy eggs exposed for even a moment. When a person approaches a nest, the female usually holds completely still, not flushing until the person is less than six

feet from her. At night, she takes occasional short breaks and also turns the eggs several times every night. About four weeks after each egg is laid, the owlet within begins making audible peeping calls and soon hatches. One mother Long-eared Owl in Idaho continued incubating an infertile clutch for at least sixty-five days as her mate continued to feed her, before a scientist finally collected the eggs.

The female stays on the nest, almost constantly brooding her nestlings until they are at least two weeks old and can maintain their body temperature without her help. At this point, she stays close to the nest all day but spends increasing amounts of time at night hunting. When the owlets are about three weeks old, before they can fly, they start leaving the nest to cling to nearby twigs and branches. For the next two weeks or so, the vulnerable "branchers" are seldom found together; scientists believe that their spreading out reduces losses to predators. The young start flying when about five weeks old; at this point they start roosting together.

Mothers remain with the family until the young are seven or eight weeks old; around this time, the young make their first attempts at hunting for themselves. Fathers continue bringing food to them for at least two or three weeks more. Sometimes two or more broods of young roost together in the same tree; it is not known whether the fathers attending to them feed any of the young that are not their own.

Researchers know very little about Long-eared Owl activities after families disperse from their nest areas. Before owl banding projects, Long-eared Owls weren't even understood to be particularly migratory. But after researchers banded thousands of owls in spring and fall along migratory pathways, it became clear that many individuals undertook seasonal movements. Since the 1970s, David Evans has banded over two thousand at Hawk Ridge Bird Observatory in Duluth. After being banded, these secretive owls are seldom heard from again—only about 1 percent of banded Long-eared Owls have ever been recovered. But of the ones banded at Hawk Ridge, Evans has had reports of twelve that were later retrapped or found dead. One that he banded in 1975 was recovered in northwestern Arkansas in December 1978, and another, banded in 1976, was found dead on a road in Manitoba in 1978. One banded at Hawk Ridge in 1973 was recovered in Puebla, Mexico, in 1977.

Long-eared Owls are listed as endangered in Illinois, as threatened in Iowa, and as a species of special concern in Wisconsin and North Dakota. So far they haven't received special protection in Minnesota and, based on Evans's numbers, are doing well. Those that manage to avoid collisions with cars and wires and encounters with mega-storms can lead fairly long lives. One banded in New York in 1989 lived to be twelve years old. ◉◉

Northern Hawk Owl

A large van filled with birders moved slowly up and down country roads near Meadowlands, Minnesota. The birders stared out the windows, their eyes intently focused on every treetop. Suddenly someone yelled, "Northern Hawk Owl!" The owl was little more than a dot, at least a hundred yards away atop a black spruce. For most of them, this wasn't just an unsatisfying view of a bird new to their life list—they weren't even sure the dot was a bird. But the driver pulled to the side of the road, and they piled out while the leader set up his scope. People lined up behind him to take a peek, but before he could even focus, the owl took off, dropping below the horizon. Two birders shrugged philosophically and headed back to the van, but another kept her binoculars trained on the bird. Suddenly she realized it wasn't flying away from them—it was winging its way across the meadow directly toward them!

It is a truth universally acknowledged that a birder in want of good birds must move slowly and be silent. But Northern Hawk Owls are functionally illiterate and haven't read this. Someone in the group shouted out the news to the people who had returned to the van, six people noisily shushed her, and the two jumping back out of the van slammed the door behind them. Yet the owl kept coming, soon so close that some people had to put their binoculars down to keep her in focus. She alighted on the power line directly above them.

Many birds from the far north are exceptionally tolerant of people. From tiny redpolls to Great Gray Owls, most northern birds have few or no encounters with people on their breeding grounds and so haven't learned to fear us. But Northern Hawk Owls, like Gray Jays, seem more than merely tolerant. They are curious about us big, two-legged mammals with our multicolored plumage. Gray Jays are nicknamed camp robbers because they so often follow large mammals, especially predators and humans, in hopes of grabbing a quick snack. No one knows for sure whether Northern Hawk Owls share the Gray Jay's instinctively optimistic gastronomic expectations, but they have been observed following farmers and forest workers to pounce on prey exposed by their equipment, and following hunters, swooping in after a shot to carry off snipe or woodcock before the hunter can retrieve them.

Some photographers toss pet store mice to owls in hopes of getting good flight shots. This is both dangerous and unethical. The Centers for Disease Control and Prevention reports that pet rodents can carry salmonella and that people in Minnesota have become sick from them; salmonella is dangerous for owls as well. Tossing a pet mouse into the snow is cruel, and if it escapes the owl, it will either be subjected to frostbite and a slow, painful death or will survive to potentially start a feral population.

Just as egregious a lapse in ethics is to use a fishing line to cast a fake mouse out, dragging it over the snow to lure the owl in for flight shots. During a harsh winter, many owls are on the very edge of death; anything we do that wastes their energy is wrong. The American Birding Association's Code of Birding Ethics states, "To avoid stressing birds or exposing them to danger, exercise restraint and caution during observation, photography, sound recording, or filming." Fortunately, Northern Hawk Owls are so tolerant that getting excellent photos of them requires little more than time and patience.

As the birders watched the owl above them on the wire, photographing her to their hearts' content, her body suddenly tensed, and her head seemed to snap to attention, her eyes locked on something they couldn't see on the other side of the roadside ditch. After a few seconds she dropped, grabbed a vole out of the snow, and returned to the power line, this time a bit farther from the crowd but still surprisingly close. Their loud exclamations of delight didn't faze her—she swallowed the rodent in one gulp, in front of everyone.

Outside of thrilling winter encounters such as this, we know very little about hawk owls, which is ironic considering how charismatic and easy to observe they are. They usually perch at the tops of trees or on power lines or poles out in the open, often using the same perches in winter that American Kestrels use in summer. Hawk owls have a strong, direct flight similar to that of falcons, and their striking facial and head markings remind some of a kestrel's. As they alight on a perch, hawk owls even bob their tail once or twice, as kestrels do. But despite the superficial similarities and sharing a similar diet of rodents, birds, and insects, the plump hawk owl would never be mistaken for the slender kestrel.

In Minnesota, the vast majority of sightings of Northern Hawk Owls take place between late December and early March. Because they spend so much time in the open and don't seem particularly wary of humans, a lot of birders get to watch them hunting, eating, and storing prey. When they capture rodents, they often fly to a perch and then swallow the animal whole, virtually always head first. Sometimes they eat the head or front half of an animal and cache the rest, often tucking it into a spruce bough or crevice. Hawk owls have been observed lopping off and swallowing the head of a red squirrel, then tearing open the side to pull out and discard the stomach and intestines before eating the rest. In Alaska, ornithologists often notice piles of discarded rodent stomachs under feeding perches.

Despite spending daylight hours in the open on conspicuous perches, Northern Hawk Owls are seldom mobbed by other birds, but occasionally birders do witness dramatic scenes. One watched a raven harassing a hawk owl for several minutes. The raven weighed at least three times as much as the hawk owl and came within inches of the owl's head repeatedly while dive-bombing it, but the feisty little predator held fast to its perch high atop an aspen until the raven finally lost interest and moved on.

Beginning in February, birders sometimes witness hawk owl courting behaviors and vocalizations. Teasing out the significance of what we see and hear isn't easy, but any time we notice two hawk owls interacting or hear one calling, it's a good idea to pay close attention, because they occasionally breed in northernmost Minnesota; nests have been found in at least five counties. In particular, keeping careful records of any calling hawk owls might help scientists and birders learn more about their breeding habits, because many ornithologists believe their calls are mostly related to courtship and nesting.

Males sing their trilling, rolling whistle, which can be heard more than a third of a mile away, beginning in mid-February and more persistently in March. They call most in early morning and in evening, both during display flights and when perched. Ornithologists believe this call is probably given to draw a female's attention to a suitable nest site. Hawk owls nest in cavities, empty woodpecker holes, open decayed hollows where treetops have broken off, and even burnt-out stumps. It's the height of rudeness to disrupt courting and nesting birds in any way. In the case of Northern Hawk Owls, it's also foolish, because they are exceptionally fierce in defending their nests.

The earliest known date for egg laying in North America is March 30. The female incubates an average of seven eggs for twenty-five to thirty days. The male appears to take an intense interest in the nest while it contains eggs or young, often trying to peek under the female and getting agitated when she leaves the nest, even briefly. He takes advantage of the long daylight hours of early summer by hunting and bringing food for his mate and their young, and storing what they don't immediately need. The young gain weight quickly, helped by those food stores. They fledge when about a month old and remain together for several weeks more. Then the family moves on, each on a separate path, bringing joy and excitement whenever one of their paths intersects ours.

Barred Owl

ho cooks for you? Who cooks for you-all?

Birdwatchers often use mnemonic tricks to help them recognize birdcalls. In most cases, people don't settle on just one choice. Does a White-throated Sparrow sing "Old Sam Peabody, Peabody, Peabody" or "Oh, sweet Canada, Canada, Canada"? Does a flying goldfinch call out "perchickory, perchickory" or "potato chip, potato chip"? We choose phrases that suggest the rhythm of the notes whether or not they make meaningful sense. Even though "Hey, sweetie!" fits both the rhythm of a Black-capped Chickadee's whistled song and the context in which it's used, many birders still remember the song as "fee-be-be" or "cheeseburger."

The one birdcall that virtually everyone remembers by the same mnemonic is the Barred Owl's "Who cooks for you? Who cooks for you-all?" The rhythm is right, and although the words are nonsensical, they somehow sound perfect. Poet Richard Wilbur described this mnemonic in his poem "A Barred Owl":

Words, which can make our terrors bravely clear,
Can also thus domesticate a fear,
And send a small child back to sleep at night
Not listening for the sound of stealthy flight
Or dreaming of some small thing in a claw
Borne up to some dark branch and eaten raw.

Barred Owls have several other vocalizations, including a deeper, slowly ascending "hoo, hoo, hoo, hoo, hoo, hoo-aw!" They often give the final, down-slurred "hoo-aw!" as a separate call. Females are larger than males, but the vocal apparatus of males is larger, producing a deeper sound. Once a calling pair has drawn close together, they often break into a duet sounding like maniacal laughter or monkeys at play. Some Barred Owls may also make this sound while subduing larger prey animals.

Barred Owls are more vocal than other Minnesota owls, and their calls have been recorded in the state during every month of the year, though most frequently in February and March. They are also more likely to call during daylight hours than other owls. Within moments of hatching, young Barred Owls start making a squeaky, hissing begging call. For the next four months, they will make that sound whenever they're hungry, while their parents continue to hoot occasionally.

Birders often try to draw in owls by imitating their voices. The Barred Owl's hoots are fairly easy for our voices to mimic, but their "monkey calls" are harder. During the early part of the breeding season, they answer our calls more readily than most owls. Once they are busy with young in late May and June, it may take many minutes for them to respond. But patience is rewarded; often they fly in to look at us before they make a sound. Calling in Barred Owls draws their attention away from their nests and young, possible meals, and potential predators, so bothering a pair more than once a season is inconsiderate.

Only two Minnesota owls have brown eyes: the Barn Owl, which is extremely rare here, and the common and widespread Barred Owl. In both species the iris is so dark that except at very close range it is usually impossible to see where iris ends and pupil begins. Barn Owls belong to an entirely different family than all other North American owls and share little else in common with Barred Owls except the first three letters of their names.

Scientists do not understand why these owls have brown eyes, nor why most owls have yellow eyes. Many, but far from all, birds of prey have yellow or orange irises, and some hawks change eye color over the course of their lives, so it is doubtful that eye color has any significant effect on vision. Songbirds seem to key in on yellow eyes when recognizing owls and cats. In the case of Barred Owls, which frequently hunt for food for their young in daytime during the time of year when parent songbirds are especially vigilant, their brown eyes might give them some relief from being bombarded by mobbing birds. On the other hand, the closely related Great Gray Owl hunts even more frequently by day yet has bright yellow eyes, and the brown-eyed Barn Owl is strictly nocturnal and spends virtually every day hidden from most birds. It's fitting that a group of birds mythologized for being mysterious hold such interesting secrets from scientists even today.

Barred Owls are generalists, hunting a wide variety of prey, including rabbits, rodents, birds up to the size of grouse, large insects, reptiles, amphibians, and even some fish. There is at least one record of a Barred Owl eating a newborn fawn while the doe was giving birth to a twin. During most of the year, Barred Owls do the majority of their hunting immediately after sunset, but when providing for a family, adult males hunt all night and occasionally throughout daytime.

A pair of Barred Owls remain together as long as they both live, staying on the same large territory year-round. They divvy up nesting responsibilities, each working around the clock during the time nestlings are tiny, but both investing pretty much the same amount of time and energy overall. The female's larger, heavier size allows her to conserve body heat more efficiently and to fight more effectively against potential nest raiders; she takes full charge of incubation and then brooding the young owlets. Sitting on one to five eggs for a full month and then keeping the chicks brooded for another two weeks might seem like an effortless and mindless task, but keeping eggs and owlets in constant warmth for so many days involves focus and huge energy expenditures. She leaves the nest to defecate and regurgitate pellets as far as a hundred yards away, making the nest difficult for birders or predators to find. She also does some hunting during incubation, but her mate provides many of her meals. Once the young hatch, he works tirelessly to provide food for the entire family, allowing his mate to do minimal hunting while the young are helpless. She spends the first two weeks brooding them, keeping the nest clean, and tearing prey that the male delivers into bite-sized morsels to feed them. Once the young are bigger and require larger meals, they are also well covered with down and capable of maintaining their body temperatures. That's when the mother too starts spending more and more of her time hunting for them.

When the owlets are four to five weeks old, they start leaving the nest, five or six weeks before they can fly. They perch on nearby branches and move about the tree by grasping at bark or twigs with their beaks as they climb about with their sharp claws, flapping their wings for balance. Eventually a great many of them fall to the ground. This is a dangerous time, but both parents remain vigilant, usually swooping and attacking intruders. The young are fairly defenseless, but when alarmed, they puff their feathers, spread their wings, hiss, and snap their beaks, making them seem larger and more dangerous. Well-meaning people often think these "branchers" need rescuing, but if left to their own devices, the young owls quickly climb into nearby trees or shrubs.

Both parents continue to feed and closely guard their chicks throughout this vulnerable stage. The young don't make their first real flights until about ten weeks of age, and it's another two weeks or so before they can make fairly long flights. The family stays together all summer. They hide out of sight as much as possible, but starting at dusk every night, and sometimes during broad daylight, nearby people can hear the young begging for food.

In fall, the parents stop feeding the young, who are growing restless for territories of their own. Once they disperse, as they chance upon the territories of other Barred Owls, the residents drive them off, but one by one the young find homes of their own, which they announce with their very own "Who cooks for you?" ◎◎

Great Horned Owl

"Mommy, look! There's a cat up a tree!" They were overdue at the child's grandparents, and there was no safe way to slow down on I-35, but the woman glanced out the window and saw the silhouette on a large limb in the snowy woodlot as they raced past. Neither she nor her son ever realized the animal they saw was not a cat but a Great Horned Owl.

This owl's upright feather tufts where a cat's ears would be, along with its general size and shape, produce a catlike silhouette, and its large yellow eyes are very cat-like. Whether songbirds are ever tricked into thinking a horned owl is a cat doesn't matter—in either case those eyes and that body shape mean danger. If a crow detects a Great Horned Owl, it yells out an "assembly call." Crows within hearing range all join in, producing their loudest, angriest-sounding caws as they swarm about the predator. Other crows from near and far produce their own assembly calls as they head toward the ruckus. The sound radiates farther and farther, bringing in more and more crows. As their numbers and noise levels increase, some crows start darting at the owl. Once in a while, one strikes the owl's head with its beak, rarely drawing blood. Large groups of crows mobbing an owl probably inspired the collective term a "murder" of crows. Crows are quicker and more agile than Great Horned Owls. As long as the crows stay above the owl's head, out of reach of talons and beak, they are safe.

Some owls tolerate mobbing more than others. One may give up and fly off to find a more secluded branch after just a few crows have appeared, but one or two crows may follow it and start the mobbing all over again. Some owls sit still throughout the ordeal, eyes half closed as if dozing unless a crow actually strikes. Other owls crouch low from the start, feather tufts pulled down and back, snapping their bill at the crows. Sometimes mobbing lasts for hours, other times for just a few minutes. Crows must balance their impulse to drive an owl away with their need to find food, attend to their young, and conduct other normal daily activities.

If crows seem merciless when attacking a roosting owl by day, the owl is far more lethal when attacking

The Great Horned Owl lives in the widest assortment of habitats with the widest geographical distribution of any North American owl. Its daytime ecological counterpart is the Red-tailed Hawk. These two birds of prey eat a much wider variety of animals than any other raptors, but in both cases seem to select the largest prey readily available. Although Great Horned Owls weigh, on average, less than three and half pounds, their talons are so powerful that as much as twenty-eight pounds of pressure is necessary to pry them open. This strength makes them especially adept at taking rabbits and hares, which may weigh as much or more than the owl. Great Horned Owls are also perhaps the only predators who specialize in skunks, which gives their feathers and sometimes the area around their nests an unmistakable odor. By weight, about 90 percent of the average Great Horned Owl's diet is mammalian, but in some areas individuals become specialists in other prey. In arid areas they may concentrate on reptiles, while in marshy areas some get the bulk of their diet from coots and ducks.

Although most Great Horned Owls weigh less than four pounds, their eyes are fully as large as an adult human's.

roosting crows by night. Crows have poor night vision and are exceptionally vulnerable after dark. Wildlife rehabilitators who need to change a dressing or administer medication to an injured crow often do it at night, when the birds are passive and helpless. A hungry Great Horned Owl can make short work of several crows while the survivors sit, rooted to their branch, silent witnesses to the carnage. Small wonder crows are so determined to drive owls away wherever they detect them.

Their eyes are also exceptionally large relative to their brain size, even compared to the eyes of other owls. The eyes are fixed, always looking directly ahead. Owls can quickly and smoothly rotate their head more than 180 degrees, and some observers report seeing captive Great Horned Owls rotate their head more than 270 degrees— in rare cases almost 360 degrees. That ability to smoothly and quickly rotate and swivel their head in every direction compensates for their inability to move their eyes. The sensory cells in their retina are mostly rods, but they do have some cones and presumably do perceive some colors. The rods are especially dense in an area of the retina, the fovea, which is above center, making their vision of objects below themselves especially acute. This is important for a bird that detects prey on the ground as it perches or flies above it. The skull juts out enough to shade the owl's eyes from bright sun.

The Great Horned Owl's hearing is most acute in the high-frequency ranges where many rodents squeak. Great Horned Owls sometimes feed on Ruffed Grouse but seldom find them while the grouse are drumming. Apparently the deep resonance of this sound is either outside the owl's hearing range, or the long wavelength makes pinpointing the direction too hard.

Female Great Horned Owls are larger and heavier than males, but males have a larger skull and produce a deeper hoot. When a pair calls back and forth, it is easy to distinguish the male from the female by his deeper voice. Great Horned Owls usually remain mated for life, which can be a long time—one individual lived more than twenty-eight years after being banded as an adult.

In Minnesota, females start laying eggs in February or March, when temperatures can still be very cold, so they must begin incubation immediately upon laying the first egg and then rarely leave the nest at all. The female can maintain her eggs' temperature at 98 degrees Fahrenheit even when the outside temperature is colder than 25 degrees below zero. In at least one case when a female joined her mate in hooting at a neighboring male, staying off the nest for twenty minutes when the temperature was 13 below zero, the eggs all survived and hatched successfully. Incubation lasts for more than a month. Her mate provides all her food during this period.

Great Horned Owl chicks hatch about two days apart, probably in the same order in which their eggs were laid. The owlets are helpless and virtually naked at hatching, so their mother continues brooding them for a few weeks as the male provides food for them all. He delivers every item to the female, who tears up even small mice for her chicks at first. At hatching, the owls weigh little more than an ounce but gain weight rapidly. By the time they are twenty-five days old, female chicks weigh more than two pounds, and males about one and three-fourths pounds. By the time the chicks are large enough to maintain their body temperature, they require more calories than a single parent can provide, so at that point the mother starts hunting too.

Unless frightened off the nest earlier by a predator, Great Horned Owl chicks start venturing out of the nest when about six weeks old, before they are capable of flight. The owlets cling tightly to tree branches, often using their beak as well as feet to balance and climb about. If they fall to the ground, they may roost there or may toddle to nearby low branches of a tree or shrub. Their parents both continue to defend them and provide food throughout the summer and early fall as the young hone their own hunting skills. As the young birds become stronger fliers, the family ventures away from the parents' defended territory. The parents continue to respond to begging calls and to defend their young into October. They finally return to their own territory after their young have dispersed.

When he returns to his territory, the male often commences hooting again, probably to defend his property. Come February, he and his mate will be duetting, and he will start bringing food to her. His valentine offerings run high to mice and rabbits at first, but with the first stirrings of warm weather, he will also be on the lookout for more fragrant offerings. Men often give women flowers; to touch a Great Horned Owl's heart, it's smarter to say it with skunks. ◎◎

Snowy Owl

One of the most famous owls in the world is a fictional character: Harry Potter's Hedwig. In J. K. Rowling's novels, Hedwig is a female, but the birds chosen to portray her in the movies have all been males. Healthy female Snowy Owls can tip the scales at over five pounds, while males weigh less than four pounds—a hefty difference that was especially significant in the early films when young Daniel Radcliffe had to carry Hedwig on his arm. Adult male Snowy Owls have another advantage in a movie about a magical world: their gleaming white plumage looks striking against black wizard robes. Female and immature male Snowy Owls are barred and speckled with dark brown.

In an iconic scene, Hedwig carries Harry's new broom, a Nimbus 2000, through the Great Hall to him. Could a real Snowy Owl succeed at such a feat? Most corn brooms weigh less than a pound and a half, while snowshoe hares and large ducks, prey for many Snowy Owls, often tip the scales at more than two pounds. So unless a Nimbus 2000's magical high-speed technology adds significantly to the broom's weight, it would be easy for a Snowy Owl to carry one. To create the movie scene, however, the owl was filmed flying through, and the broom was added digitally.

Real Snowy Owls live in open terrain from just above the tree line to the edge of the polar seas in North America, Europe, and Asia. Every winter, some wander south from Canada and Alaska to the Great Plains, and at least a few appear annually in Minnesota. They can be found anywhere in the state, but the single most reliable place to find them is the Duluth harbor. David Evans, who bands raptors at Hawk Ridge Bird Observatory every autumn, has been studying the Snowy Owls in the Duluth–Superior area every winter since 1974. During the 1970s and early 1980s, when spilled grain from shipments through the harbor supported a large population of Norway rats, the owls were especially abundant; Evans caught and banded one or two dozen every year, and one winter he banded thirty-three. Now that rat numbers are lower, he averages about ten Snowy Owls a year.

During some winters, in what we call invasion years, Snowy Owls appear in large numbers throughout the northern and even central United States. Some of these birds are underweight or even starving, but researchers have discovered that most have reasonable fat levels and that some of the starving individuals bear old injuries, usually from collisions with wires or automobiles, which have impaired their ability to hunt.

Snowy Owl invasion years tend to coincide with cyclic periods of low abundance for lemmings. These feisty, hamster-sized Arctic rodents form the bulk of Snowy Owl diets; some Snowy Owls eat little else. Ornithologists used to explain owl irruptions as simple cause and effect, and many contended that few of these owls ever return to their Arctic homes because so many apparently starve or are killed while south of their breeding grounds. But banding studies by David Evans and others established that some individual Snowy Owls return to a wintering area year after year, surviving not just one entire season and the return trip to the Arctic but several more. Now ornithologists realize that Snowy Owl distribution is more complex than their original boom-and-bust model explained. The birds that wander the farthest tend to be young males; adult females, the largest and most capable of defending a winter territory against competitors, remain the farthest north. Apparently unless food is abundant, young males are forced to wander when larger, more aggressive Snowy Owls evict them from their winter territories.

Once they reach Minnesota, Snowy Owls spend most of their time in open areas, virtually never in forests. On the tundra, Snowy Owls don't experience branches above their heads. Trees near the tundra tend to be short conifers with branches so densely packed that a four- or five-pound owl can easily sit atop them. Perhaps that's why when they retreat to Minnesota they rarely sit in trees. The slow but steady northward advance of trees associated with climate change may expand the range of Great Horned Owls at the expense of Snowy Owls.

Snowy Owls are adept at grabbing ducks, and whether in the north or south, they gravitate to icy shorelines. Because people and industry also gravitate to lakes and rivers, a surprising number of Snowy Owls spend their winters in major cities. Birders yearning to see these splendid icons of Arctic wilderness may be disappointed to see their "lifer" atop a railroad car, rooftop, or sign rather than in a beautiful natural setting. More Snowy Owls are reported each year in three urban areas—Duluth-Superior, Milwaukee, and Madison—than in the rest of Minnesota and Wisconsin combined. When they were most abundant in the Duluth harbor, Evans witnessed territorial defense and hooting by wintering Snowy Owls, but few birders observing them in winter ever hear them vocalize at all.

Birds that nest in "the land of the midnight sun" must be adept at hunting in daylight or their young would starve; they also must be able to hunt at night or they themselves would starve during the long, dark Arctic winter. When they retreat to Minnesota, Snowy Owls are sometimes seen hunting in daylight but are far more active at dawn and dusk, when crows, ravens, and Peregrine Falcons are less likely to spot them. The most dramatic stories of Snowy Owls in Duluth involve interactions with the peregrines that nest in town. Often a peregrine dive-bombs an owl over and over, flying in at high speed and veering off just before impact. Sometimes the owl jumps and lunges with its feet extended toward the falcon, but this may incite the falcon to attack even more aggressively. Sometimes these encounters last for several minutes. Evans has observed this many times during his decades of raptor research but has never seen a peregrine actually hit or injure a Snowy Owl. This behavior may be an example of play on the peregrine's part. Snowy Owls and Peregrine Falcons don't compete directly for food, peregrines seldom scavenge or steal carcasses killed by owls, and Snowy Owls aren't known to kill peregrines, so there doesn't seem to be any real advantage to the peregrine in battling them. But attacking Snowy Owls may be an instinctive behavior to drive away owls in general because the Peregrine Falcon's only major predator is the Great Horned Owl.

Minnesota's Snowy Owls start heading north again beginning in late winter. Stragglers are occasionally seen in May, and back in 1890, one was reported in Meeker County in June.

Nesting on the tundra begins in May. The female uses her claws to scratch out a shallow depression on the ground. Despite the permafrost, she is not known to add any insulating materials. Windswept areas are preferred, apparently to keep snow from drifting and collecting near the nest.

When food is limited, her clutch may consist of three to five eggs, but when food is plentiful, she may lay as many as seven to eleven. She sits tight on the nest virtually constantly during the thirty-one days it takes for the first egg to hatch as her mate guards her and provides food. Once the eggs begin hatching, she spends more time standing up, picking apart the animals her mate brings her and feeding morsels to the chicks. The first to hatch gets the lion's share, but when food is abundant, all the nestlings can survive. In one nest of eleven eggs, all the eggs hatched, and at least ten of the chicks successfully fledged.

Despite the harsh environments in which they live and the dangerous migrations they undertake, wild Snowy Owls can live well over a decade. One female banded in Massachusetts in 1988 lived to be almost seventeen years old, enduring more than sixteen years of fierce Arctic weather and at least three long-distance migrations. She was still going strong right up until she was killed in an airplane collision.

Great Gray Owl

The owl perched on a tiny tamarack branch, staring at one spot on the ground below, his ears, hidden behind huge facial disks, listening for the tiniest squeak or rustle beneath the snow. The birder pulled over, got out of the car, and stood transfixed. The owl looked up and met her eyes but within seconds turned to gaze at the ground again.

A smooth, thick layer of new snow covered the field, and the birder couldn't see anything different in the spot where the owl was looking than anywhere else, but the owl continued staring. A logging truck roared past, but he didn't move a muscle. Suddenly he opened his huge, silent wings and took off, directly toward the invisible spot. He hovered above it a moment, then crashed into the snow, face and feet first, and was still. The birder's heart pounded. But then the owl opened his vast wings again, pushed off against the snow, and took off, leaving behind a beautiful snow angel. His feet dangled, grasping a plump brown meadow vole. He flew straight back to the snow-covered tamarack. He landed so lightly that the branch barely stirred, but snow on the branch bounced into motion like fairy dust. He looked at the birder for such a short moment that she wondered if she had imagined it. Then he hunched over, took the vole into his mouth, and swallowed it in a single practiced motion. He met the birder's eyes again and then turned to stare at a new spot on the ground.

The birder felt exhilarated, thrilled beyond measure, her heart full, her soul stirred by this magical moment that would be seared in her memory forever. But for the owl, this was a typical winter day, this meal like any other. Indeed, meadow voles comprised the vast majority of his diet day after day, season after season, year after year. Some days he didn't catch more than one or two, but on a good day he could eat as many as seven. As long as voles kept stirring and the birder remained quiet and kept her distance, irritating though her presence might be, he would stick around until his stomach was full.

The Great Gray Owl is the largest owl in North America, and one of the largest owls in the world, as measured with a ruler. But the Snowy Owl and Great Horned Owl are both significantly heavier. Some healthy male Great Gray Owls weigh a mere one and a half pounds, and some emaciated individuals that recover weigh half that—less than three-fourths of a pound. A Great Gray Owl is feathers and spirit and not much more.

Why must such lightweights appear so large? Their size allows them to reach prey buried under eighteen inches of snow, and their huge wings allow them to pull out again. But even when voles are abundant, they can't supply enough nutrition to sustain a body as massive as a Great Horned Owl's. And such massive muscularity would be excess baggage for a bird who doesn't need to overpower anything as large as a grouse or rabbit. Because voles are so tiny compared to most animals taken by Great Horned and Snowy Owls, Great Gray Owls don't need their powerful talons either. A Great Gray Owl's toes and claws are long, giving it a broad grasp to better grab at unseen prey. But as wildlife rehabilitators and banders quickly figure out, the talons of even healthy, wild Great Gray Owls don't pack much of a punch. These birds can often be handled without protective gloves.

Great Gray Owl eyes are smaller and their ears larger than those of Snowy and Great Horned Owls. Even

when not hidden beneath snow, meadow voles are seldom seen from above ground; in summer they live within grassy tunnels. It is likely that Great Gray Owls never see most of their prey at all until the voles are firmly in their grasp.

Great Gray Owls usually sit near the top of the American Birding Association's "Most Wanted" list, the species birders most yearn to see. In 1973, over three thousand birders descended on a farm in Massachusetts just to see a Great Gray Owl wintering there. Minnesota birders take them a little more for granted because Great Grays live year-round in northeastern Minnesota. The many birders regularly scouring Aitkin County and the boggy part of St. Louis County near Meadowlands and Cotton (an area nicknamed the Sax-Zim Bog) provide precise locations on hotlines. Birders doing "Big Years" generally spend a few January or February days in northern Minnesota to add this and other northern owls, Boreal Chickadees, and various northern finches to their list.

During the winter of 2004-5, northern Minnesota experienced an unprecedented invasion of Great Gray Owls, which made national news. In December, one birder counted 250 in a single day. By early January, at least 1,700 birds had been reported in the state. By May, over

700 dead Great Gray Owls were packed into museum drawers and freezers, and experts estimated that as many as 10,000 Great Grays had descended upon the state. Although the vole population in northern Minnesota was extremely low during summer 2004, the owls weren't necessarily starving. All of the 39 Great Grays admitted that winter to the Raptor Center in St. Paul had suffered collisions with automobiles, and all were judged to be in good physical condition prior to being injured.

That winter, many people observed Great Gray Owls eating much larger prey than voles. One was observed staring into a hole in the ice above a roadside stream. Twice when a muskrat surfaced to take a breath, the Great Gray dropped down and successfully grabbed and pulled it out of the water. One Duluth neighborhood that had been overrun with domestic rabbits became a reliable place to observe the owls. After killing a rabbit, owls were often observed sitting on the carcass for forty-eight hours or more, guarding and keeping it from freezing as, little by little, the owl stripped away the meat. In a few cases, Great Gray Owls were even observed eating dead Great Grays. Some species of owls regularly kill their own species for food when stressed by hunger, but since these Great Grays were usually observed at roadsides, it is more likely they were eating birds that had been killed by cars.

It is unlikely we will ever experience such a huge influx of Great Gray Owls again in our lifetimes, but they continue to be regularly seen in the state. They are easiest to find in winter, but breeding birds can be found too, usually nesting in old hawk and raven nests. One pair raised three or four young in a crow nest barely large enough to accommodate the growing owlets.

When the vole population is stable, Great Gray Owls may select the same mate year after year. In the western United States, where Great Grays are rather sedentary, pairs probably remain together as long as both survive, but in the boreal forest regions of Canada and Minnesota they do more wandering and don't maintain their pair bond over the winter.

Great Gray Owls are usually silent outside of the nesting season. Both sexes give the territorial call: several deep, resonant, evenly spaced hoots we humans perceive as ethereal and haunting. A series of double hoots may serve as contact calls between a pair. In winter, birders who hear a Great Gray Owl snap its bill or hiss are usually approaching much too closely to an owl guarding a hard-won meal. Seeing them even from a distance is thrilling. Giving them a little space so they can eat in peace is not just a courtesy: it's the right thing to do. ◎◎

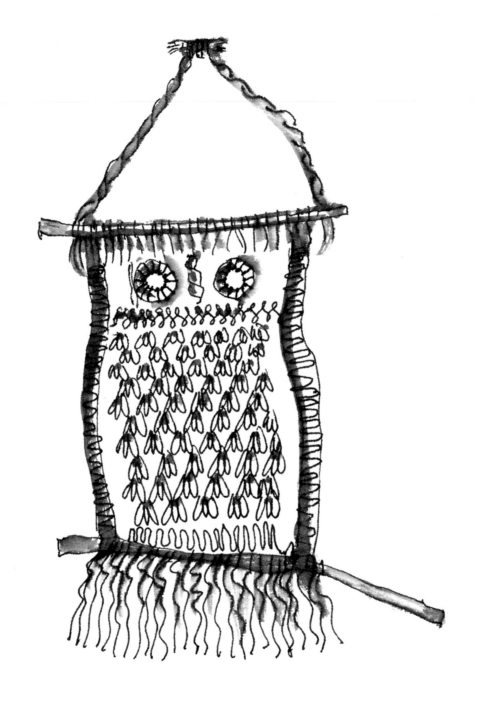

Laura Erickson has been writing and speaking about birds, and promoting their conservation, for thirty-five years. Her daily radio spot and iTunes podcast "For the Birds" airs nationally, and she has written four previous books about birds, including *Sharing the Wonder of Birds with Kids,* which received the National Outdoor Book Award.

Betsy Bowen is a renowned woodcut printmaker and painter. She has illustrated several books, among them *Great Wolf and the Good Woodsman, Borealis, Wild Neighborhood,* and *Big Belching Bog,* all published by the University of Minnesota Press. She lives in Grand Marais, Minnesota.